Ilona Chovancova

pies without pastry

Photographs by Hiroko Mori

contents

Duck

Fish

Sundry

Vegetable mash toppings

Potato mash

5 large potatoes • ½ cup crème fraîche or light cream • ½ cup milk • 2 tablespoons/¼ stick butter • salt and freshly ground black pepper

Peel the potatoes and cut into pieces. Boil in salted water until tender but not overcooked. Drain and mash, using a potato masher, handheld blender, or a ricer for a smoother mash. Add the crème fraîche or cream, milk, and butter and season to taste with salt and pepper.

Sweet potato mash

5 or 6 sweet potatoes • ½ cup light cream • 2 tablespoons/¼ stick butter • 1 garlic clove, crushed • 2 teaspoons paprika • salt and freshly ground black pepper

Peel the sweet potatoes and cut into pieces. Boil in salted water until tender but don't overcook, then drain and crush coarsely using a potato masher. Add the cream, butter, garlic, and paprika and season to taste with salt and pepper.

Sunchoke mash

2 lb sunchokes (Jerusalem artichokes) • ½ cup crème fraîche or light cream • ½ cup milk • 2 tablespoons/¼ stick butter • salt and freshly ground black pepper

Peel the sunchokes and remove the "knobs," or scrub, and cut into pieces. Boil in salted water until tender but don't overcook. Drain and coarsely crush using a potato masher. Add the crème fraîche or cream, milk, and butter and season to taste with salt and pepper.

Pea purée

about 1¼ lb frozen peas • 4 tablespoons crème fraîche or light cream • 2 tablespoons/¼ stick butter • 1–2 tablespoons chopped mint (optional) • salt and freshly ground black pepper

Cook the frozen peas according to the instructions on the packet, then drain and mash into a purée using a potato masher or handheld blender. Add the crème fraîche, or cream, and butter, stir in the chopped mint, if using, and season to taste with salt and pepper.

Celeriac mash

1 celeriac (celery root) • 1 tablespoon balsamic vinegar or lemon juice • salt and freshly ground black pepper

Peel the celeriac and cut into pieces, cook in boiling salted water until tender but don't overcook, then drain and crush coarsely using a potato masher. Add the balsamic vinegar or lemon juice and season with salt and pepper.

Eggplant mash

4 eggplants • 4 tablespoons crème fraîche or plain yogurt • 1–2 tablespoons finely chopped parsley • 1 tablespoon lemon juice • salt and freshly ground black pepper

Either bake the eggplants in a preheated oven at 400°F for 20 minutes and leave to cool, or prick with a fork and microwave for 15 minutes (or follow the oven-maker's instructions). Cut the cooked eggplants in half and scoop out the flesh with a spoon. Purée the flesh in a blender along with the crème fraîche or yogurt, mix in the parsley and lemon juice, and season with salt and pepper.

Zucchini mash

2 onions, sliced • olive oil • 6 zucchini, scrubbed and finely diced • ½ cup crème fraîche or plain yogurt • salt and freshly ground black pepper

Fry the onions in a little olive oil, add the zucchini and season with salt and pepper to taste. Add a little water, cover and simmer gently for about 20 minutes. The zucchini must be thoroughly cooked but not mushy. Remove from the heat, drain if necessary, and mash using a potato masher. Stir in the crème fraîche or yogurt.

Carrot mash

5 carrots • 2 potatoes • ½ cup light cream • 2 tablespoons/¼ stick butter • 1¼ cups grated cheese • 1 pinch of ground cumin • 1 tablespoon lemon juice • 1 teaspoon pink peppercorns • salt and freshly ground black pepper

Peel the carrots and potatoes and cut into even-sized pieces. Place in a large pan of salted water, bring to the boil and simmer until tender but don't overcook. Drain and crush coarsely using a potato masher, then briefly return to the hob over a low heat to evaporate any excess water. Remove from the heat and add the cream, butter, grated cheese, cumin, lemon juice, and pink peppercorns. Season with salt and pepper to taste.

Pumpkin purée

1 lb pumpkin flesh • butter or duck fat • ¼ cup grated Parmesan cheese • 1 tablespoon ground cinnamon • salt and freshly ground black pepper

Remove the seeds and dice the pumpkin flesh. Fry in a little butter or duck fat for about 10 minutes. Add a little water, cover and continue to cook until the pumpkin is very soft, remove from the heat and purée using a potato masher or handheld blender. Add the Parmesan cheese and cinnamon and season to taste with salt and pepper.

Beet purée

4 beets • 4 tablespoons crème fraîche or plain yogurt • 1 tablespoon lemon juice • salt and freshly ground black pepper

Preheat the oven to 400°F. Wash the beets, but do not peel and place in a roasting pan with a splash of water or olive oil. Cover tightly with foil and bake for 1–1½ hours (depending on size), until tender but not mushy (test by piercing with a skewer). When the beets are cool enough to handle, peel then purée in a blender with the crème fraîche or yogurt and lemon juice. Season to taste with salt and pepper.

Basic cottage pie

Serves 4

knob of butter

2 onions, finely chopped

1 lb ground beef

1–2 tablespoons chopped parsley

salt and freshly ground black pepper

For the topping

5 large potatoes

2 tablespoons/¼ stick butter

½ cup milk

½ cup crème fraîche or light cream

salt and freshly ground black pepper

Make the potato mash topping following the recipe on page 4.

Melt the butter in a pan and brown the onion and ground beef, breaking up any lumps. Then allow to cook for 5 minutes, stirring frequently.

Remove from the heat, add the parsley, and season with salt and pepper.

Preheat the oven to 350°F.

Grease an ovenproof dish and add a layer of potato mash followed by a layer of meat. Top with a second layer of potato mash and bake for 20 minutes. The top should be nicely browned and crispy.

Tip To add a special touch, fry sliced onions in some butter and a little sugar until caramelized and spoon over the cooked pie.

Cottage pie made with beef and beet purée

Serves 4

Serves 4

2 lb stewing beef

1 tablespoon oil

2 carrots, peeled and sliced

2 garlic cloves, finely chopped

1 bottle red wine (or 3 cups water)

2 shallots or 1 onion, chopped

1 piece of celeriac (celery root), or a rib of celery, cut into pieces

2 thyme sprigs

2 bay leaves

salt and freshly ground black pepper

For the topping

4 cooked beets (see page 5), diced

4 tablespoons crème fraîche or plain yogurt

1 tablespoon lemon juice

salt and freshly ground black pepper

Cut the meat into cubes. Heat the oil in a pan and brown the meat on all sides. Add the carrots and garlic and fry with the meat for a few minutes. Add the wine, or water, followed by the shallots, celeriac and herbs. Season with salt and pepper, cover and simmer over low heat for 3 hours.

Meanwhile, make the beet purée topping as described on page 5.

Preheat oven to 350°F.

When the meat is tender, leave it to cool slightly before shredding, using 2 forks. Transfer the shredded meat to a greased ovenproof dish, top with the beet purée and bake for 20 minutes.

Tip Beet purée is also delicious served with a little horseradish or with fresh herbs, such as dill, parsley or basil.

Cottage pie with sun-dried tomatoes

Serves 4

2 tablespoons olive oil

1½ lb ground beef

a few sun-dried tomatoes in oil

1 garlic clove, crushed

2–3 tablespoons chopped pine nuts

1–2 tablespoons chopped basil

salt and freshly ground black pepper

For the topping

5 large potatoes

2 tablespoons/¼ stick butter

½ cup milk

½ cup crème fraîche or light cream

salt and freshly ground black pepper

Make the potato mash topping following the recipe on page 4.

Heat the oil in a pan and brown the ground beef, then cook for 5 minutes, stirring frequently to break up any lumps.

Drain and dice the sun-dried tomatoes. Remove the pan from the heat, and add the tomatoes to the meat together with the garlic, pine nuts and basil. Season with salt and pepper.

Preheat the oven to 350°F.

Grease an ovenproof dish and place a layer of potato mash in the bottom. Follow by a layer of meat, top with a second layer of potato mash and bake for 30 minutes. The top should be brown and crispy.

Tip **Add a few fresh aromatic herbs to the potato mash.**

Beef and celeriac pie

Serves 4

2 lb stewing beef

2 garlic cloves

2 onions, chopped

4 carrots, peeled and sliced

1 celeriac (celery root), cut into large pieces

4 leeks, white part only, trimmed, cleaned, and sliced

2 thyme sprigs

1 bay leaf

1 tablespoon oil

salt and freshly ground black pepper

For the topping

the celeriac, which has been cooked with the meat

1 tablespoon balsamic vinegar (or lemon juice)

salt and freshly ground black pepper

Place the beef in a large casserole, cover with cold water and bring to a boil. Remove any scum as it forms, using a slotted spoon. Season with salt and pepper.

Lower the heat and cook for a further 40 minutes. Add the garlic, vegetables and the herbs, and simmer over gentle heat for a further 1½ hours, checking the celeriac regularly.

When the celeriac is cooked through but not mushy, remove it with a slotted spoon. Make the celeriac mash by crushing coarsely with a potato masher. Add the balsamic vinegar or lemon juice and season with salt and pepper.

Preheat the oven to 350°F.

Set aside the meat to cool slightly before shredding it, using 2 forks. Add the cooked vegetables, if you like, and spread over the base of a greased ovenproof dish. Top with the celeriac mash and bake for about 20 minutes, or until the topping is nicely browned.

Tip **For a change, make this pie with sunchoke mash (see recipe on page 5).**

Cottage pie, Thai-style

Serves 4

1 tablespoon olive oil

2 lemongrass stalks, sliced

1 lb ground beef

2 red onions, sliced

2–3 tablespoons chopped basil

2–3 tablespoons chopped mint

3 tablespoons nuoc mam (Thai fish sauce), or lemon juice

salt and freshly ground black pepper

For the topping

5 large potatoes

2 tablespoons/¼ stick butter

½ cup milk

½ cup crème fraîche or light cream

salt and freshly ground black pepper

Make the potato mash topping following the recipe on page 4.

Heat the oil in a pan and fry the lemongrass stalks.

Add the ground beef and cook for 5–10 minutes, stirring frequently to break up any lumps.

Remove from the heat, add the onions, herbs, fish sauce or lemon juice, and season with salt and pepper.

Preheat the oven to 350°F.

Grease an ovenproof dish, add a layer of potato mash followed by a layer of meat, then top with a second layer of potato mash and bake for 30 minutes or until the top is nicely browned and crispy.

Tip If there is any meat left over, it is also delicious served cold accompanied by a salad of arugula leaves.

Chicken and spinach potato pie

Serves 4

1 roast chicken, meat shredded

For the spinach purée

1 lb fresh leaf spinach (or 10 oz frozen spinach)

1 generous knob butter

2 eggs

3/4 cup ricotta or other soft sheep's milk cheese

2 tablespoons crème fraîche or plain yogurt

1 tablespoon pine nuts

pinch of grated nutmeg

salt and freshly ground black pepper

For the topping

5 large potatoes

2 tablespoons/1/4 stick butter

1/2 cup milk

1/2 cup crème fraîche or light cream

salt and freshly ground black pepper

Make the potato mash topping following the recipe on page 4, adding 2–3 tablespoons of the spinach mixture to the potato mash if you wish.

Wash the spinach, remove the stalks and shake dry.

Melt the butter in a sauté pan. Add the spinach and fry for about 10 minutes.

Leave to cool and thoroughly strain off any remaining liquid.

In a mixing bowl, beat together the eggs, cheese, and crème fraîche or yogurt. Add the spinach, pine nuts, and nutmeg and mix well. Season with salt and pepper.

Preheat the oven to 350°F.

Grease an ovenproof dish, add a layer of half the potato mash followed by a layer of chicken, then a layer of spinach purée, and a final layer of the remaining potato mash. Bake in the preheated oven for 30–40 minutes.

Curried smoked chicken and potato pie

Serves 4

oil, for frying

1 onion, finely sliced

1 smoked chicken, meat shredded

2 tablespoons curry paste

2 tablespoons crème fraîche or plain yogurt

1 tablespoon chopped dill

salt and freshly ground black pepper

For the topping

5 large potatoes

2 tablespoons/¼ stick butter

½ cup milk

½ cup crème fraîche or light cream

1 teaspoon finely chopped dill

salt and freshly ground pepper

Make the potato mash topping following the recipe on page 4. Add the finely chopped dill.

Heat the oil in a pan and fry the onion, then add the shredded chicken and the curry paste. Leave to simmer for 5 minutes, remove from the heat, and add the crème fraîche or yogurt and the dill. Season with salt and pepper.

Preheat the oven to 350°F.

Grease an ovenproof dish, add a layer of half the potato mash followed by a layer of chicken, top with a second layer of potato mash and bake for 20 minutes until the top is nicely browned and crispy.

Chilean chicken and potato pie

Serves 4

1 tablespoon olive oil

1 onion, sliced

1 roast chicken

6 corn cobs, cooked, kernels removed and coarsely chopped (or 2½ cups canned corn, drained and coarsely chopped)

¾ cup milk

2 tablespoons brown sugar

3 eggs, separated

butter, for greasing

salt and freshly ground black pepper

Heat the oil in a pan and fry the onion. Shred the chicken meat, using 2 forks, and add to the onion. Leave to simmer for a few minutes. Season with salt and pepper.

Place the corn in a bowl, add the milk, sugar and egg yolks. Season with salt and pepper and mix well together.

In another bowl, whisk the egg whites into stiff peaks, and carefully fold into the corn mixture.

Preheat the oven to 350°F.

Grease an ovenproof dish, add a layer of chicken, and top with the corn mixture. Bake for 30 minutes. The top should be nicely browned and crispy.

Tip For people with a sweet tooth, sprinkle the surface of the pie with sugar and place under a hot broiler until caramelized.

Rabbit and polenta pie

Serves 4

1 tablespoon olive oil

1 prepared rabbit, jointed

3/4 cup chicken stock

1 lb fresh figs, diced

1 rosemary sprig

2 tablespoons honey

1 tablespoon balsamic vinegar

1 1/3 cups instant polenta

2 cups milk

salt and freshly ground black pepper

Heat the oil in a pan and brown the rabbit pieces all over. Add the stock, cover and leave to simmer for 30 minutes, turning the rabbit pieces once or twice, adding a little more stock or water if necessary. Add the figs, rosemary and honey and leave to simmer, uncovered, for 10 minutes. Season with salt and pepper and add the balsamic vinegar.

Meanwhile, cook the polenta in the milk, following the makers instructions on the packet.

Preheat the oven to 375°F.

When the rabbit is cooked, leave it to cool slightly. Shred the meat, using 2 forks, and stir into the fig mixture. Grease an ovenproof dish, add a layer of half the polenta followed by a layer of rabbit and figs. Top with the remaining polenta and bake in the oven for 10 minutes until nicely browned.

Rabbit pie with goats' cheese mash

Serves 4

2 tablespoons oil

1 onion, finely sliced

1 garlic clove

1 prepared rabbit, jointed

¾ cup chicken stock

1 cup canned chopped tomatoes, or 4 fresh tomatoes, peeled and diced

a few sage leaves

2 tablespoons/¼ stick butter

salt and freshly ground black pepper

For the topping

5 large potatoes

2 tablespoons/¼ stick butter

½ cup milk

½ cup crème fraîche or light cream

4 oz strong flavoured goats' cheese, diced

handful snipped chives

salt and freshly ground black pepper

Make the potato mash topping following the recipe on page 4, adding the diced goats' cheese and snipped chives.

In a large, heavy pan, heat the oil and fry the onion and garlic. Add the rabbit pieces and brown on all sides. Stir in the stock, tomatoes and sage, cover and leave to simmer for 30 minutes, turning the rabbit pieces once or twice. Season with salt and pepper.

When cooked, leave to cool slightly, then shred the meat using 2 forks.

Pre-heat oven to 375°F.

Grease an ovenproof dish, spread a layer of half the potato mash over the base and add a layer of the rabbit mixture. Top with a second layer of potato mash and bake for 20 minutes until the topping is brown and crispy.

Lamb and eggplant pie

Serves 4

1 small (or half) leg or shoulder of lamb

⅔ cup olive oil

4 garlic cloves, sliced lengthwise

handful chopped thyme

salt and freshly ground black pepper

For the topping

4 eggplants

4 tablespoons crème fraîche or plain yogurt

handful finely chopped parsley

1 tablespoon lemon juice

salt and freshly ground black pepper

Preheat the oven to 400°F.

Make the eggplant mash topping following the recipe on page 4.

While the eggplants are cooking, prepare the lamb. Rub the joint well with the olive oil. Using a sharp, pointed knife, make incisions in the lamb and insert a garlic slice in each one. Sprinkle with the thyme and season with pepper.

Place the lamb in a roasting pan containing ¾ cup water and roast for about 1 hour, basting frequently with the cooking juices. Season with salt 15 minutes before the end of the cooking time.

Remove the lamb from the oven and reduce the temperature to 350°F. Leave the meat to cool slightly, then shred with 2 forks and place in a greased ovenproof dish. Top with the eggplant mash and bake for 30 minutes.

Tip Eggplants are easy to cook in a microwave oven (see recipe on page 4). Instead of parsley, add some other aromatic herbs such as basil, chervil or thyme in the eggplant mash.

Shepherd's pie with minted peas

Serves 4

1 small (or half) leg
or shoulder of lamb

²/₃ cup olive oil

4 garlic cloves, sliced
lengthwise

handful chopped thyme

salt and freshly ground
pepper

For the topping

¼ lb frozen peas

4 tablespoons crème
fraîche or plain yogurt

2 tablespoons/¼ stick
butter

1–2 tablespoons chopped
mint

salt and freshly ground
black pepper

Make the pea purée topping following the recipe on page 4.

Preheat the oven to 375°F.

Rub the lamb well with the olive oil. Using a sharp, pointed knife, make incisions in the lamb and insert a garlic slice in each one. Sprinkle with the thyme and season with pepper.

Place the lamb in a roasting pan containing ¾ cup water and roast for about an hour, basting frequently with the cooking juices. Season with salt 15 minutes before the end of the cooking time. Remove the meat and reduce the oven temperature to 350°F.

Leave the meat to cool slightly, then shred, using 2 forks, and place in a greased ovenproof dish. Top with the pea purée and bake for about 15 minutes or until the top has formed a crisp crust.

Tip For a change, why not add other aromatic herbs such as parsley, basil or chervil to the pea purée instead of the mint, or even sprinkle the pie with crispy broiled diced bacon.

Greek shepherd's pie

Serves 4

1 tablespoon olive oil

1 onion, sliced

1 garlic clove, crushed

3 zucchini, finely diced

1 lb ground lamb

7 oz feta cheese, finely diced

2–3 tablespoons chopped mint

salt and freshly ground black pepper

For the topping

5 large potatoes

2 tablespoons/¼ stick butter

½ cup milk

½ cup crème fraîche or light cream

salt and freshly ground black pepper

Make the potato mash topping following the recipe on page 4.

Heat the oil in a pan and fry the onion and garlic, add the zucchini and the ground lamb and leave to simmer for 5 minutes. Remove from the heat and add the feta cheese and the mint. Season with salt and pepper and stir until all the ingredients are thoroughly incorporated.

Preheat oven to 350ºF.

Grease an ovenproof dish, add a layer of half the potato mash, followed by a layer of the lamb mixture. Top with a second layer of potato mash and bake for 30 minutes. The top should be nicely browned and crispy.

Tip For a change, try making this pie with zucchini mash (see recipe on page 4) instead of potato mash.

Fowler's pie

Serves 4

3 conserved duck thighs, (available in some delicatessens or by Internet mail-order)

3 shallots, chopped

1 garlic clove, crushed

8 oz wild/exotic mushrooms, chopped

1–2 tablespoons chopped parsley

salt and freshly ground black pepper

For the topping

5 large potatoes

2 tablespoons/¼ stick butter

½ cup milk

½ cup crème fraîche or light cream

salt and freshly ground black pepper

Make the potato mash topping following the recipe on page 4.

While the potatoes are boiling, quickly fry the duck in a skillet to take off the fat, reserving a little for frying the shallots, garlic, and mushrooms. Remove the skin and fat from the duck and then shred the meat, using 2 forks.

Fry the shallots and garlic in a little of the reserved duck fat, then add the mushrooms. Remove from the heat, add the parsley, and season with salt and pepper.

Preheat oven to 350ºF.

Grease an ovenproof dish. Fill with alternate layers of potato mash and duck, then top with a layer of mushrooms and bake for 20 minutes.

Tip For a really festive pie, use duck or goose liver and celeriac mash (see recipe on page 4) garnished with truffles.

Potato-topped confit of duck with onion and apple

Serves 4

3 conserved duck thighs, (available in some delicatessens or by Internet mail-order)

3 Russet, Braeburn or Granny Smith apples, diced

2 tablespoons lemon juice

2 onions, finely chopped

salt and freshly ground black pepper

For the topping

5 large potatoes

2 tablespoons/¼ stick butter

½ cup milk

½ cup crème fraîche or light cream

salt and freshly ground black pepper

Make the potato mash topping following the recipe on page 4.

Quickly fry the confit of duck in a skillet to take off the fat, reserving a little for frying the onions. Remove the skin and fat from the duck and then shred the meat, using 2 forks.

Peel, core, and chop the apples. Place in a mixing bowl and add the lemon juice.

Fry the onions in a little of the reserved duck fat. Add the apples and the duck. Cover and leave to simmer for 20 minutes, then season with salt and pepper.

Preheat the oven to 350°F.

Grease an ovenproof dish and add a layer of half the potato mash followed by a layer of meat. Top with a second layer of potato mash and bake for 20 minutes or until the topping is nicely browned.

Tip You can also make this pie with fruits such as peaches, figs, grapes or pears instead of the apples, depending on the season.

Duck and pumpkin pie

Serves 4

3 conserved duck thighs, (available in some delicatessens or by Internet mail-order)

For the topping

1 lb pumpkin flesh

1 tablespoon ground cinnamon

¼ cup freshly grated Parmesan cheese

salt and freshly ground black pepper

Make the pumpkin purée topping following the recipe on page 5.

In a skillet, quickly fry the confit of duck to remove the fat. Remove the skin and fat from the duck and then shred the meat, using 2 forks. Season with salt and pepper.

Preheat the oven to 350ºF.

Grease an ovenproof dish, add a layer of half the pumpkin purée followed by a layer of duck, then top with a second layer of pumpkin purée and bake for 15 minutes.

Tip **For a more substantial topping, stir some potato mash into the pumpkin purée.**

Duck pie with conserved tomatoes

Serves 4

3 conserved duck thighs, or a 600-g can confit of duck

1 lb vine-ripened cherry tomatoes (preferably still on the branch)

2 garlic cloves, crushed

1–2 tablespoons chopped thyme

1 tablespoon sugar

salt and freshly ground pepper

In a skillet, quickly fry the confit of duck to remove the fat, reserving a little of it. Remove the skin and fat from the duck, shred the meat with 2 forks, and add the sugar.

Preheat the oven to 350°F.

Place the shredded meat in a greased dish and arrange the cherry tomatoes on top. The tomatoes will look even more attractive and will keep their shape better if you keep the vine branches on. Sprinkle with the garlic, thyme and sugar, and drizzle with a little of the reserved duck fat. Season with salt and pepper.

Place in the oven and bake for about 1½ hours, basting frequently with the remaining duck fat.

Tip **Serve with potato mash (see recipe on page 4) or simply with a salad of arugula leaves.**

Mixed meat and potato pie

Serves 4

leftover chicken

leftover duck

leftover stewed beef

2 tablespoons oil

2 onions

1 garlic clove, crushed

1–2 tablespoons fresh herbs such as parsley, chives, tarragon, thyme or mint, finely chopped

salt and freshly ground black pepper

For the topping

5 large potatoes

2 tablespoons/¼ stick butter

½ cup milk

½ cup crème fraîche or light cream

salt and freshly ground black pepper

Make the potato mash topping following the recipe on page 4.

Shred the meat, using 2 forks, or cut into dice. Heat the oil in a pan and fry the onions, then add the meat and garlic. Leave to simmer for 5 minutes, then remove from the heat, and add the finely chopped fresh herbs. Season with salt and pepper.

Preheat the oven to 350°F.

Grease an ovenproof dish, add a layer of half the potato mash followed by a layer of meat, then top with a second layer of potato mash and bake for 20 minutes or until the top is nicely browned.

Blood pudding and potato pie

Serves 4

1 tablespoon oil

2 onions, sliced

10 oz chestnuts, chopped

1 lb blood pudding

salt and freshly ground
black pepper

For the topping

5 large potatoes

2 tablespoons/¼ stick
butter

½ cup milk

½ cup crème fraîche or
light cream

salt and freshly ground
black pepper

Make the potato mash topping following the recipe on page 4.

Heat the oil in a sauté pan and fry the onions and chestnuts for 2–3 minutes. Remove the casing from the blood pudding and fry the contents with the onions and chestnuts, breaking up any lumps. Season with salt and pepper.

Preheat the oven to 350°F.

Grease an ovenproof dish and add a layer of half the potato mash followed by a layer of the blood pudding mixture, then top with a second layer of potato mash and bake for about 30 minutes, until the top is brown and crisp.

Tip You can make this pie with apples, grapes or other fruit of your choice instead of the chestnuts.

Fish pie with sweet potato paprika mash

Serves 4

1½ lb white fish fillets

2 tablespoons lemon juice

salt and freshly ground
black pepper

For the topping

5–6 sweet potatoes

½ cup light cream

2 tablespoons/¼ stick
butter

1 garlic clove, crushed

2 teaspoons paprika

salt and freshly ground
black pepper

Make the sweet potato mash following the recipe on page 4.

Preheat the oven to 350°F.

Put a layer of half the sweet potato mash in a greased ovenproof dish.

Cut the fish fillets into small pieces and arrange them on the layer of sweet potato. Sprinkle with the lemon juice and season with salt and pepper.

Top with a layer of the remaining sweet potato mash and bake for 20 minutes.

Fish pie with carrot mash

Serves 4

1½ lb cod, or other white fish, fillets

2 tablespoons olive oil

2 tablespoons lemon juice

salt and freshly ground black pepper

For the topping

5 carrots

2 potatoes

½ cup light cream

2 tablespoons/¼ stick butter

1¼ cups grated cheese

1 pinch of ground cumin

3 tablespoons lemon juice

1 teaspoon pink peppercorns

salt and freshly ground black pepper

Make the carrot mash topping following the recipe on page 5.

Preheat the oven to 350°F.

Place the fish fillets in a dish, sprinkle with the olive oil and lemon juice and season with salt and pepper. Bake for 20 minutes or until cooked through but not overcooked. Remove the fish from the oven but leave the oven on.

Leave the fish to cool slightly before flaking it with a fork.

Grease an ovenproof dish and add a layer of half the carrot mash followed by a layer of fish. Top with a second layer of carrot mash and garnish with the reserved pink peppercorns. Return to the oven for about 20 minutes to brown.

Tip As an alternative, use 1 teaspoon of grated fresh ginger or 1–2 tablespoons of chopped fresh herbs, such as tarragon, chives or parsley, instead of the pink peppercorns.

Salmon and potato pie with chopped vegetables

Serves 4

2 carrots, sliced

1 fennel bulb, diced

2 leeks, trimmed, cleaned and sliced

2 tablespoons olive oil

1½ lb salmon pieces

2 tablespoons lemon juice

¾ cup crème fraîche or plain yogurt

1 egg

salt and freshly ground black pepper

For the topping

5 large potatoes

2 tablespoons/¼ stick butter

½ cup milk

½ cup crème fraîche or light cream

salt and freshly ground black pepper

Make the potato mash topping following the recipe on page 4.

In a pan, fry the carrots, fennel and leeks in the oil and season with salt. Add a little cold water, cover and cook for 20 minutes, then remove from the heat.

In a mixing bowl, combine the salmon pieces with the lemon juice and season with salt and pepper.

Beat together the crème fraîche or yogurt and the egg, season with salt and pepper and stir into the vegetables.

Preheat oven to 350°F.

Grease an ovenproof dish and add a layer of the vegetable mixture followed by a layer of salmon, then top with a layer of potato mash and bake for 40 minutes.

Tip **Alternatively, stir the salmon into the vegetable mixture.**

Brandade de morue (salt cod) and potato pie

Serves 4

1¾ lb salt cod fillets,
soaked to remove the salt

1 large garlic clove

1¾ cups olive oil

¾ cup milk

1 tablespoon lemon juice

freshly ground black pepper

For the topping

5 large potatoes

2 tablespoons/¼ stick
butter

½ cup milk

½ cup crème fraîche or
light cream

salt and freshly ground
black pepper

To remove the salt, soak the salt cod fillets in cold water for 12 hours before preparing the dish, changing the water several times.

Make the potato mash topping following the recipe on page 4.

Drain the cod fillets and place in a pan. Cover with cold water, bring slowly to a boil, then lower the heat and poach for 10 minutes.

Drain the fish, shred the flesh, using 2 forks, and remove the bones. Coarsely crush the garlic clove, add to the fish and beat with a wooden spoon. Add the olive oil a little at a time, beating constantly. As soon as the oil is absorbed, add a little milk and continue beating. Add the lemon juice and season with pepper.

Preheat oven to 350°F.

Grease an ovenproof dish, add a layer of half the potato mash followed by a layer of salt cod mixture, top with a second layer of potato mash and bake for 20 minutes. The top should be nicely brown and crispy.

Tip The filling of this pie, called brandade de morue in France, is delicious with the addition of a few black olives. If you have any of the filling left over, spread it on slices of toast made from a crusty country loaf and serve as a canapé.

Cod with sweet and sour red cabbage

Serves 4

2 tablespoons olive oil

3 onions, finely sliced

1 tablespoon brown sugar

½ red cabbage, finely sliced

1 teaspoon ground cumin (optional)

1 bay leaf

½ cup cider or balsamic vinegar

2 lb cod fillets, or any similar white fish

2 tablespoons lemon juice

salt and freshly ground black pepper

For the topping

5 large potatoes

2 tablespoons/¼ stick butter

½ cup milk

½ cup crème fraîche or light cream

salt and freshly ground black pepper

Heat 1 tablespoon of the oil in a pan and fry the onions. Add the sugar and continue to cook until the onions begin to caramelize. Add the red cabbage, cumin, bay leaf, and vinegar. Cover and simmer over a low heat for 1 hour, adding a little water if the mixture becomes too dry before the cabbage is cooked. Season with salt and pepper.

Make the potato mash topping following the recipe on page 4.

While the red cabbage is cooking, prepare the fish.

Preheat oven to 350ºF.

Arrange the fish fillets in an ovenproof dish, sprinkle with the lemon juice and remaining olive oil and season with salt and pepper. Bake for 20 minutes or until the fish is cooked through. Set aside to cool slightly then flake the fish with a fork, removing any bones.

Using the same dish, build up alternate layers of potato mash, red cabbage and fish. Return the dish to the oven and bake for 15 minutes.

Tip If you can find a jar of ready-prepared red cabbage (but not the pickled variety), just heat it up and season to taste.

Cod and potato pie with lentils and pesto

Serves 4

1 generous cup Puy lentils (French green lentils)

1 onion, sliced

1 garlic clove, chopped

2 bay leaves

1³/₄ lb cod fillets, or other firm white fish

3 tablespoons lemon juice

1 tablespoon olive oil

3 tablespoons pesto

2 tablespoons basil, coarsely chopped

1 tomato, peeled and diced

salt and freshly ground black pepper

For the topping

5 large potatoes

2 tablespoons/¹/₄ stick butter

¹/₂ cup milk

¹/₂ cup crème fraîche or light cream

salt and freshly ground black pepper

Cook the lentils together with the sliced onion, garlic and bay leaves in a large pan of gently boiling salted water for 25–30 minutes.

Meanwhile, make the potato mash topping following the recipe on page 4.

Preheat the oven to 350°F.

Arrange the fish fillets in a dish, sprinkle with the lemon juice and olive oil, season to taste with salt and pepper and bake for 20 minutes, or until cooked through.

Drain the lentils and stir in the pesto, basil, and tomato and season lightly with salt and pepper.

When the fish is cooked, leave it to cool slightly before flaking the flesh. In the same dish, build up alternate layers of potato mash, fish and lentils, then return to the oven for 15 minutes to brown.

Tip For a lighter dish, omit the potato mash and just make the pie with the fish and lentils.

Chorizo and black olive potato pie

Serves 4

1 lb chorizo sausage

3/4 cup pitted black olives

freshly ground black pepper

For the topping

5 large potatoes

2 tablespoons/1/4 stick butter

1/2 cup milk

1/2 cup crème fraîche or light cream

salt and freshly ground black pepper

Make the potato mash topping following the recipe on page 4.

Remove the skin from the chorizo sausage and cut the sausage into pieces. Process with the olives and a little pepper in a blender to form a purée.

Preheat oven to 350°F.

Grease an ovenproof dish and fill with the chorizo and olive mixture topped by potato mash. Bake in the preheated oven for 20 minutes until brown.

Tip You can make this pie with sun-dried tomatoes instead of olives, or alternatively serve the chorizo and olive mixture spread on slices of toast.

Bacon and red kidney bean potato pie

Serves 4

8 oz smoked bacon, diced

15 oz can red kidney beans

1 tablespoon crème fraîche

salt and freshly ground black pepper

For the topping

5 large potatoes

2 tablespoons/¼ stick butter

½ cup milk

½ cup crème fraîche or light cream

salt and freshly ground black pepper

Make the potato mash topping following the recipe on page 4.

Fry the diced bacon in its own fat in a skillet until crispy. Rinse and drain the red kidney beans, add to the bacon, cover and cook for about 10 minutes.

Remove from the heat and crush the beans with a fork. Stir in the crème fraîche and season with pepper.

Preheat the oven to 350°F.

Grease an ovenproof dish and add a layer of half the potato mash followed by a layer of the bean and bacon mixture. Top with a second layer of potato mash. Bake for 20 minutes until the top is crisp and brown.

Artichoke heart and red bell pepper pie

Serves 4

1 tablespoon olive oil

8 oz frozen or canned artichoke hearts, finely diced

2 red bell peppers, finely diced

1 garlic clove, crushed

1 pinch of ground cumin

salt and freshly ground pepper

For the topping

5 large potatoes

2 tablespoons/¼ stick butter

½ cup milk

½ cup crème fraîche or light cream

salt and freshly ground black pepper

Make the potato mash topping following the recipe on page 4.

Heat the oil in a pan and fry the artichokes and peppers until soft. Add the garlic and cumin and season to taste with salt and pepper.

Preheat the oven to 350°F.

Grease an ovenproof dish and add a layer of potato mash, top with a layer of the artichoke and pepper mixture and bake for 15 minutes.

Tip You can serve this dish as an accompaniment or as a main meal with a salad.

Red pesto and puréed pea pie

Serves 4

For the red pesto

1 jar sun-dried tomatoes in oil

1 red bell pepper

1 good handful of pine nuts

1 tablespoon olive oil

salt and freshly ground black pepper

For topping

about 1¼ lb frozen peas

3 tablespoons crème fraîche or plain yogurt

salt and freshly ground black pepper

Process all the pesto ingredients together in a blender. Season to taste.

Cook the peas according to the recipe on page 4, leaving out the mint.

Preheat the oven to 350°F.

Grease an ovenproof dish and add a layer of half the puréed peas followed by a layer of red pesto Top with a second layer of puréed peas and bake for 15 minutes.

Tip You can use a variety of different vegetables for the purée, such as potatoes, broccoli, carrots, or pumpkin instead of peas.

© Marabout 2003

Reproduction: Reproscan

This edition © Hachette Livre (Hachette Pratique) 2005
This edition published by Hachette Illustrated UK, Octopus Publishing Group Ltd.,
2–4 Heron Quays, London E14 4JP

English translation by JMS Books LLP (email: moseleystrachan@aol.co.uk)
Translation © Octopus Publishing Group Ltd.

A CIP catalogue for this book is available from the Library of Congress

ISBN 10: 1 84430 159 1

ISBN 13: 978 1 84430 159 1

Printed by Toppan Printing Co., (HK) Ltd.